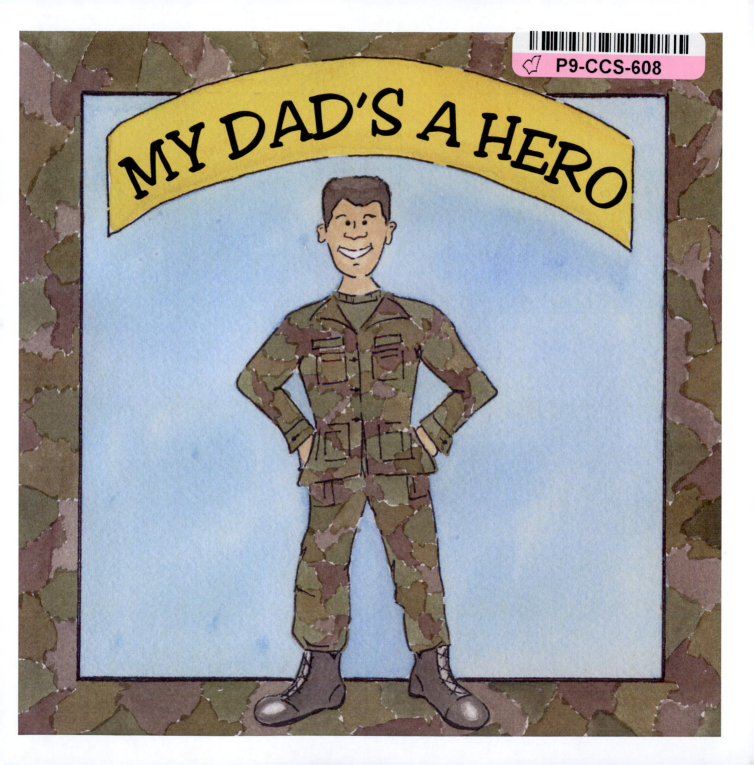

MY DAD'S A HERO

by Rebecca Christiansen & Jewel Armstrong

Illustrations by Jen O. Robertson

Word Association Publishers
www.wordassociation.com

Printed in the United States of America.

ISBN: 978-1-59571-209-7
Library of Congress Control Number: 2007934472

Word Association Publishers
205 5th Avenue
Tarentum, PA 15084
www.wordassociation.com

To all the moms, dads, and children
who have become heroes.

Dad, you will always be our hero.
Easton & Gracee

MY DAD'S A HERO

Paste photo of your dad here

My dad works for the United States military. He wears a flag on his uniform that stands for freedom...

...but that's not what makes him a hero.

No costumes, capes or flashy colors, my dad's uniform is camouflage. Camouflage means he can blend into his surroundings just like a chameleon. He is very good at hiding...

...but that's not what makes him a hero.

My dad uses lots of special equipment,
a helmet, big boots, even goggles that
help him see in the dark...

...but that's not what makes him a hero.

Many heroes work for the military, on the land, in the sky and on the oceans. My dad wears dog tags around his neck that shows everyone his name...

...but that's not what makes him a hero.

My dad and I send photos and letters to each other. I keep his picture on the dresser by my bed. When I miss my dad, looking at pictures of him makes me feel better.

I like to draw happy things for him
to look at when he misses me.
He says my pictures always
make him smile.

to DAD

My dad gets to drive and ride in
Humvees, tanks, airplanes, helicopters,
ships and very big trucks...

...but that's not what makes him a hero.

My dad lives with more heroes on a military base or in a big tent. He sleeps on a cot or bunk bed while he's away.
He is very good at camping...

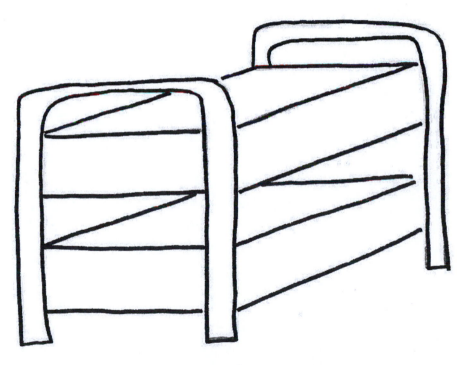

...but that's not what makes him a hero.

When my dad feels hungry he gets to eat M.R.E.'s, which are meals ready-to-eat. My dad says some of them come with candy, but he would rather have pancakes with me...

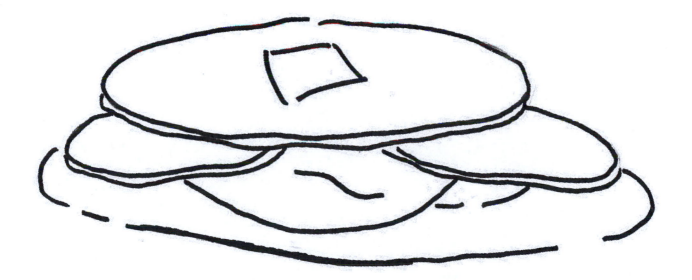

...but that's not what makes him a hero.

Sometimes my family sends my dad videos of the things we are doing here at home. I sent him a really cool video of my birthday party so he wouldn't miss it.

My dad loves me very much.

My dad and other military heroes help people in different places build roads, schools and hospitals. In the hospitals they help the sick get well so they can return to their families...

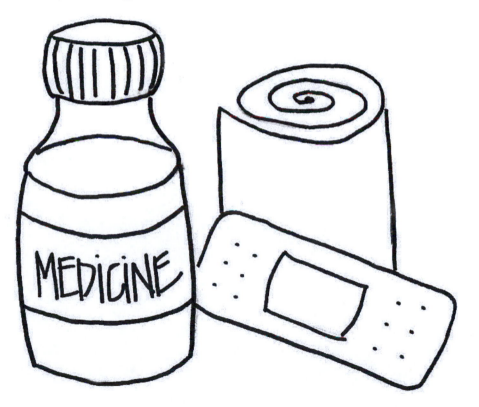

...but that's not what makes him a hero.

The United States military protects people all around the world. My dad travels to far away lands to help bring peace and create hope for the people living there...

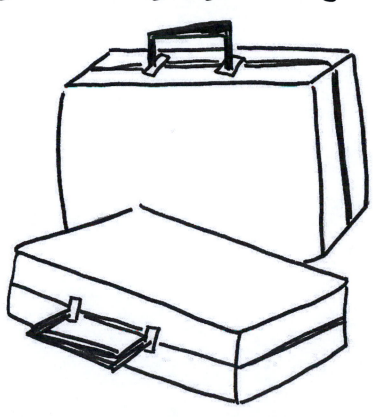

...but that's not what makes him a hero.

Whenever my dad gets the chance he calls me on the phone to talk. He has to be gone such a long time and hearing his voice is like getting a big hug.

I know my dad will be back soon.

While my dad is away, we hang a flag and a yellow ribbon to remind us and our friends that he is doing very hard hero work. My dad wants all people to have the chance to live a happy life...

...but that's not what makes him a hero.

I am very excited for my dad to come home. My family and I are preparing a big party for the day of his return...

...but that's not what makes him a hero.

When my dad comes home he will get to be in a big parade, everyone will cheer and celebrate. My family is very proud of my dad...

...but that's not what makes him a hero.

There are many hero words like save, help, build and bravery. The most important hero word is sacrifice. Sacrifice means to give up.

My dad gives up some birthdays, some holidays, and some other fun times. My dad sacrifices his time with me and my family to help those in need.

This sacrifice is what makes him a HERO.

I love my dad very much. I am willing to sacrifice time with him, because I know he is helping so many other families.

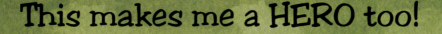

This makes me a HERO too!

I AM A HERO

Paste your photo here.

Rebecca, Jen, Jewel

Meet the Creators

I was inspired to write a book for my children, Easton and Gracee, when my husband was deployed. I teamed up with my good friend Jewel, who is also my son's teacher and together we wrote this book. Through her extensive work with young children and my military background we felt we were able to create a book that was very positive, age-appropriate, and personalized for each child.

Once the book was written, we joined forces with Jen, another friend, to illustrate. Through her lively and meaningful illustrations she was able to capture the emotion of the story and really brought the book together. Our shared hope in creating this book is that it will be a tremendous source of strength for you and your child. We hope you will find it to be a pleasure to read, and a book that will give your child an understanding of what their dad does in the military.

We want each child who reads this book to know what sacrifice means, that their dad is a real life hero and most importantly that they are a hero too.